LIVE

OUT OF THE

ZONE

Live life the way you want

SURAJIT CHAKRAVARTY

This is dedicated to the dreamer.

Someone who dares to dream & wants

to achieve it no matter how big it is.

Author's note

Why did I write this book?

This book is for those people, who are living in a zone of life at this time, they don't like living in that zone. And they want their dreams to be a reality, which is in a different zone. And the way they are living their life presently is a different zone. They do not understand how to get out of this zone, enter into their dream zone, and live in that zone permanently. And how to get everything as quickly as possible that does not exist in the zone, they are currently living in.

My sole purpose in writing this book is that whatever obstacles I faced in turning my dreams into reality, other people should get easy ways to deal with such obstacles on the way to their success. So that as soon as possible they can live their life in their dream zone, and they can easily do the work they want, and become whoever they want to be.

Whether you want to earn a lot of money or you want to do something big in life, or you want to have a better relationship, or you want to be a doctor, lawyer, actor, businessman, cricketer, singer, whatever. If you are not living the way you want to live then you are living your life in a different zone, where you do not like to live in. This book is a direct way to step out of the same zone and live in your dream zone forever.

Why does this book matter to me?

Since childhood, I was always curious to know the answer to a question. Why whatever one wants, he gets it easily? Home, money, wealth, car, and his desired life partner, anything. And some people do not get this much even if they want. After all, why? Is god kinder to some people of this world, and less kind to some people? Why are some people very lucky, and some unlucky? Why do some people get a lot by doing a little hard work and some people do not get anything special even after working hard? Those answers to these simple questions have been written in detail in this book. I hope this book will guide the generations to come to live life the way they want.

CONTENTS

Chapter 1

Getting out of the loop

GETTING OUT OF THE LOOP

"The thinking brain influences the body's responses and it makes a neat little loop"-Brad Warner

There is a total of 7.9 billion people in this world. But everyone is living in their zones. There is a lot of money in someone's life, and there is everything they want, and people call them rich. If someone has less money, they call them middle class, and if someone doesn't have any money, they call them poor. But everyone has different behaviour, different interests, different type of friends, different likes and dislikes, a different way of thinking, and different points of view. This means in any situation, whether it is good or bad, everyone's point of view to look at the situation is different. In short, we all live in different zones. We all have created our separate zone. In every aspect of life, we all have different likes and dislikes. In any situation, we all react differently. We just go through the days according to our set zones and go on walking without questioning whether this zone is right for me or not. We look at any situation in a way that may or may not happen. According to someone's belief, something may be impossible but it does not mean that it is true. This is just someone's belief. Maybe someone else is looking at this problem differently, and it is indeed possible. The work which we consider impossible for ourselves, we start thinking subconsciously that, the work will be impossible for everyone in this world. We all get caught in a mental loop living with the same beliefs, and many other such false beliefs. And that becomes our reality. It becomes programming in our minds. And whatever happens in our life, every action of ours is being done because of this programming only. Most people are getting stuck in this loop, and keep following this mental programming. And they do not even realize that their life is constantly spinning in the same loop. But they think that they are poor only because their luck is bad. And they believe that this is what was written in their destiny so this is what they are getting. They often blame the government, that they are poor because of the government. They think that statesman took away their rights; the government is not giving them jobs so they are poor, but the truth is far from it. They don't even realize that it is nobody else but they are creating it. And they stay stuck in the loop constantly.

How to get out of the loop?

You'll have to reconstruct your belief system and question it. You have to be mindful of what you believe in and what you don't.

Suppose, you live in a very small village and now you are 30 years old. And your journey so far has been more painful in poverty. That's why subconsciously there is programming in your mind that you are poor, and you can never become rich. This programming exists because of your belief system. All the rich or successful people you see are successful today because they were never in this mental loop. And if by mistake also they ever got into this loop, then they got out of this loop early. So, if you want to get out of this loop then you have to change your belief system first. You have to convince yourself that you can become anything. And you can achieve anything. And this has to be done every day. When we are determined to achieve anything, from that very moment that thing becomes ours. After that, all we need is to take the necessary actions.

But most people don't think like that. They are not determined to do what they want. And they give up. That's why their dream doesn't turn into reality.

You have to resort to positive affirmations. Affirmations are a very powerful tool to rebuild your belief system. Affirmations are some positive talks that you speak to yourself in your mind. If negative thinking is always going on in your mind, as if you can never live your dream life, you can't do this, you can't do that etc, instead, you can repeat the positive affirmations that everything is possible, you can do anything, and you can achieve anything no matter how big or tough it seems now. By repeating it, again and again, your subconscious mind starts believing those positive talks. And your mind will be reprogrammed. Then your every belief, every action, your attitude of looking at everything becomes like the new programming of your mind, and you will start coming out of the loop.

Chapter 2

Gratitude is the highest vibration

GRATITUDE IS THE HIGHEST VIBRATION

"The struggle ends when the gratitude begins"-Neale Donald Walsh

If you want to understand the universe thinks in terms of energy, frequency, and vibration.-*Nikolas Tesla*. We all vibrate at a certain frequency. The whole universe is governed by emotion. We have some positive feelings which make us feel good, and have some negative feelings which make us feel bad; if you keep feeling positive continuously then you will always be in a positive vibration, and vice versa. If good things happen in your life, and you come in contact with good people, then your life is considered very happy and beautiful. And if unwanted things happen in your life, and if you come in contact with not so good people, then your life is considered unhappy. Now the question is how to make every moment according to your mind.

If we want to make our life more positive then we have to make our vibration positive first. Then only we can live our life according to our minds. ***Gratitude is at the top of all the positive vibrations.***

Why do we get something and from where?

There is an infinite intelligence from which we get everything. Some people consider it as a god, creator, divine, and almighty. People of such different beliefs consider it by different names. The same Infinite Intelligence governs the entire universe. And from this infinite intelligence, everything is made. Everything you see in this universe today, the Sun, the Moon, planets, solar system, galaxies, humans, animals, plants, cars, buildings, wealth, everything comes from the same source. Apart from this, everything you have now also came from the same source. If you have deep gratitude, you can be in harmony with that source. If you want to convert your unwanted life into the life you want, then it is imperative to achieve this harmony.

The only problem is when you get what you want; you don't express gratitude to that supreme intelligence. You forget the source only, from which you got what you wanted. The result is that you stop getting good things ahead.

When you are grateful to the Infinite Intelligence for what you have got, then you are always in harmony with that source. The result is that whatever you want, moves towards you even faster. And you go up the ladder of prosperity. There will be no mistakes in doing work. Because infinite intelligence also keeps working with you.

How to express gratitude effectively?

Whatever you receive every day, small or big, if you have any good experiences, you can express your deepest gratitude to Infinite Intelligence. Often, we go to god only when we have a bad time or we need something that we are not getting. As soon as we get the thing asked for, we forget the source from which we have got that thing. On attaining every little, and big thing or experiencing the desired situation, if you express your deepest gratitude to the almighty, then you will be constantly in the highest vibration. And in this situation, it becomes very easy to get anything for you, no matter how big it is. Your paths will start opening up, and you will start getting closer to your goal. You will be surprised that what you are doing so differently nowadays, which you did not do before, and because of this good things are happening to you. If you look carefully around you, you will find that many people are like this. They get everything very quickly. And some people do not get anything special even after trying and working hard. This is because some people always are in positive vibrations, and some people are not. Because of not understanding this, most people struggle.

The benefits of gratitude are not only this much that it will give you the most boon in the future. Rather if there is no gratitude, then you feel an unsatisfied desire for what you do not have. And the same unsatisfied desire goes into your subconscious mind; the result is that you start getting unwanted things in large numbers. If you focus on unwanted things, you will get unwanted things only. Because what you focus on is what you get.

Gratitude creates faith. And without faith, you can't get everything you want easily.

Some people do all the work but in the absence of gratitude, they are not able to achieve anything special.

Chapter 3

Thoughts are things

THOUGHTS ARE THINGS

"We are what we think"-Gautam Buddha

You must be thinking about how thoughts are things. If I ask you that if you jump ten times from a tall building without a parachute, how many times will you fall, and how many times will you go up? If your answer is ten times only you will fall, then you understand the law of gravity very well. The Law of gravity is a law of nature, and no one can change it. Similarly, there are many other laws of nature, and all those laws are also very accurate, and no one can change them. One of those laws of nature is what you think you will get. Every great person in this world had differences in every other opinion. But all of them were absolutely the same on one thing that man becomes what he thinks.

Every person in this world has complete freedom to think about the things he wants. What to think is completely in the hands of man. But as he keeps thinking, so will he become. 96% of the world's money is earned by 1% of the world population. It is not a coincidence at all. The thought of money is always on their mind. As a result, their life is always full of money. On the contrary, those who have a lack of money or poverty in their mind, get more and more of the same. When we think of something for the first time, it is an idea. When we think about it 2-3 times, it becomes a thought. And when we think of that thought, again and again, it becomes our belief. And then we start attracting circumstances of the same way in our life as we believe.

The only problem is we think more and more about what we don't have. We usually think this way, 'I don't want to live in poverty, or I am struggling, or I don't have this or that, or my life is miserable'. You keep looking at the same thing over and over again that you don't want. Apart from thinking that I don't want to live in poverty, you can think that I want to live like rich.

If you think of poverty, you will only have poverty. We often create negative thinking by looking at the obstacles. Example – 'I don't have money or I don't have the resources, so I can't do this or she won't let me do this, or it's the thinking of the rich, we poor cannot think like that.

It is much easier for a person to think negative than to think positive. And that's why most people think negatively. But if we want, we can stick with our positive thinking. When we think negatively, then our belief also becomes negative. And then our whole life becomes like that. Whatever experiences you have had in your life so far, whatever has happened in your life, whether it is good or bad, whatever situation you are in at this moment, it is only because of your thinking.

If you are anxious, scared or worried about a particular result, then you are creating more and more bad situations.

When the situation keeps getting worse then people start thinking that their luck is bad. But the truth is far from this.

Whatever you criticize, whether it is illness, circumstances, enmity, or whatever, you are bringing the same thing into your life.

The only difference is that you are not fully consciously observing what you are thinking, and what is happening in your life because of it.

If your thinking is positive then only positive situations will come in front of you. And if your thinking is negative then only negative situations will come in front of you.

If you want to change the circumstances of your life, then the easiest way is to change your thoughts. Whenever a negative thought comes into your mind, ignore it. Think only about the things, and situations you want. And then unwanted things will disappear from your life as if they were never there.

Chapter 4

Staying in the inner world ignoring
the outer

STAYING IN THE INNER WORLD IGNORING THE OUTER

"When your inner world comes into order your outer world will come into order"-I Ching

Whatever situation you are living in right now is not your reality. Maybe you're living in a smaller house right now, you don't have enough money, don't have a favourite life partner, and you are not living life the way you want to live. This is just the result of your old thoughts and deeds. We are constantly living as the result of our old thoughts and deeds. And when we attach ourselves to the present situation, we punish ourselves for being in this situation in the future as well.

If you believe everything you want to happen happened, then gradually you will start attracting similar situations as per your belief. And your every action will start happening in the same way as your belief. And sooner or later you will be able to completely emerge from the old situation, and your life will begin to transform. You will start attracting the same things into your life as your inner world will be. And you will be surprised that why you are taking so many intense actions to live your dream life as you have never taken before. Your inner world means a world has to be created in your mind. Your dream world. Exactly how you want your life to look. And you can use your imagination to do this. You have to visualize your dream life with all your senses. And whatever is going on in the world outside your mind, and whatever circumstances you are in right now, all those things have to be ignored. By which very soon your dream will turn into reality. And your old outer world will gradually change, and your inner world will be transformed into the outer world.

We don't get what we want, we get what we are. Whatever world is in your mind, you attract similar things into your life. If you have in your mind the corresponding thing of your present outside world, like lack of money, Worst relationship status etc, then you will attract more things of the same way in your life. And apart from this, if you focus on the world you want, and consider it as your reality, then according to that world you will attract things in your life. It doesn't matter what you tell people about yourself. It only matters what you think about yourself inside your mind.

Most people always pretend in front of others that I am this or I am that. But in reality, they keep thinking negatively about themselves. Like I can't become this, I can't do this etc. It will not be of any use. It only matters what you say in your mind, not what you say to others on the outside.

Chapter 5

Imagination is the doorway to the future

IMAGINATION IS THE DOORWAY TO THE FUTURE

"Imagination is everything.it is the preview of life's coming attractions"- Albert Einstein

If there is anything in this world that has not been fully understood, it is the mind. The mind has infinite potential. Our brain remembers images easily. In the time of primitive man, man did not have any language; they used to think about anything by imagination. Before the Wright brothers were making the aeroplane, it was in their imagination. It was in Nikola Tesla's Imagination before the alternating current was invented. Before the telephone invention; it was in the imagination of Alexander Graham Bell.

Whenever you imagine something, you embody it. This is a simple way to explain to Infinite Intelligence what we want. When you imagine anything clearly in your mind, similar situations you find in your real life. Due to not understanding this thing, many people are not able to get what they want. Every time they ask for things from Infinite Intelligence with their own words. But one word has many meanings. That is why it is very important to imagine so that Infinite Intelligence can understand what you want after all. Then the easiest and most effective ways to achieve your goal will keep coming to your mind in the form of ideas, and if you keep taking action according to those ideas, you will keep moving forward.

When you imagine your dream and leave an impression in the subconscious mind, then people's minds will start getting affected everywhere; everyone will start to turn your dream into reality. Everyone starts working for you even though they don't realize it. From the moment you imagined your dream with all your senses as if it had come true, so sooner or later it will become a reality. There is no such question that it should not be fulfilled, as long as you keep taking action according to your instinct. After that, you'll start attracting everything you need. To fulfil your dream, you just have to work on every idea that you will get, and you have to keep moving forward making decisions quickly.

How do imagine effectively?

Suppose you want to become a very big businessman so you can imagine this way, how you are sitting in your chamber in an office. You are well dressed. And you have an expensive watch in your hand; there is a laptop on the table. How your employees are working in the office; their voices will also have to be heard in your imagination. You also need to imagine how your office looks from the inside. Need to look at every detail very closely. And you have to feel the joy that you will feel when you will become like this. And after assuming that you got all this in reality, you have to give sincere thanks to infinite intelligence. This will make it much easier to get what you imagined. Your path will start opening up. Ideas will keep coming to your mind, and then you will also have to take necessary actions. And in this way, you can turn your dreams into reality.

Chapter 6

Utilizing the power of the subconscious-mind

UTILIZING THE POWER OF THE SUBCONSCIOUS-MIND

"Whatever we plant in our subconscious mind and nourish with repetition and

emotion will one day become a reality"-
EARL NIGHTINGALE

What is the subconscious mind?

One part of our mind is always conscious of everything in the outside world. It is called the conscious mind. And one part is always conscious about everything in the inside world; it is called the subconscious mind. The subconscious mind is the part of our brain that manages our body. Like heart beating, liver functioning, digestive system working, and lots of things in our body are maintained by the subconscious mind. Apart from these things, there is other work of the subconscious mind as well. Like remembering memories of the past, remembering every habit, to store our dreams, beliefs, thoughts, ideas, and according to those thoughts and beliefs, it creates situations in our life. This means that whatever thoughts we let into our subconscious mind, similar situations start happening in our life. When a person learns to drive, for the first time he learns through the conscious mind. And after that with every practice, this information about driving gets stored in the subconscious mind. After that man never forgets to drive. In the same way, every activity of your life, every skill, habit, thought, feeling, dream, your goal, is constantly piling up in your mind. But all this will only go into your subconscious mind when you allow any thought or habit through your conscious mind to enter into the subconscious mind. As if you're looking at a flower right now, only your conscious mind knows this. Your subconscious mind won't know until you tell it what you're seeing.

You must have heard people talking about not being stressed in difficult times. It is said so because your subconscious mind does not know that something bad has happened. So that the subconscious mind does not create a worse situation than this. Although, people say it unknowingly to give sympathy.

Your subconscious mind is a powerful tool, if you fit any idea, goal, dream, then it will turn into reality. No one can stop it. It's like a double-edged sword. This means it cannot differentiate between positive and negative thoughts. This means that every thought you sow, whether it is positive or negative, will turn into reality, no matter whether it benefits or harms you.

To explain this, we can take the example of soil and farmer. You can think of the soil as the subconscious mind, and consider yourself to be a farmer. You sow whatever you want in it. What to sow is completely in your hands. If you sow positive seeds, then your subconscious mind will create positive situations. And if you sow negative seeds, it will bring only negative situations in your life. It is entirely in your hands what to sow in your subconscious mind. What you sow will create your reality. You can test it. If you go to sleep at night by telling your subconscious mind that you want to wake up tomorrow at 6 am. So, you will see that the next day you will automatically get up before 6 o'clock without an alarm. The subconscious mind is bound to obey your every command. This way you can make anything, and any situation you want. Our subconscious mind controls every single movement of ours. That's why we have to take special care of what information we let go into our subconscious minds. Because our subconscious mind can make us and can also destroy us.

Chapter 7

Thinking in terms of successful people

THINKING IN TERMS OF SUCCESSFUL PEOPLE

"Successful people tend to become more successful because they are always thinking about their success"-Brian Tracy.

There will be many challenges in front of you as you move forward while working towards your dream life. Then it will depend only on your thinking that you will overcome those challenges and move forward or you will remain the same.

Suppose you are walking home from the office, and somewhere 2000 rupees note accidentally fell from your pocket, now you don't know where it fell. Will you regret that note now? Due to this your valuable time will be wasted, and your energy will be spoiled. In the time when you could have earned that money back by doing some other work. At that time whenever you have a bad feeling, you can think of an example of a very successful person. You can take the example of any successful person; can be a famous cricketer, celebrity, businessman, or singer. Example: You can think this way, 'if this money had fallen from Mr Bill Gates today, would he have regretted it today?' If the answer comes from within you that 'he won't', then ask yourself, 'if he doesn't think like that then why am I thinking like this?' Because I also want to make my life successful.

When you keep thinking about every situation in this way, then gradually you will have the ability to handle every situation. And you will get the ability to take the right decision in every situation. You will become unstoppable. Then no situation can beat you. Because no situation can defeat you until you lose yourself. You can think like a successful person in every situation. Then you will start to feel as if the same successful people are taking all your decision, and you will be able to move towards your goal very fast. People usually look at the people around them who are not successful. And think like them. They often say 'I'm doing it because everybody does it like that'. But they don't even realize that the 'everybody' they are following is the average class. They always follow people who are part of the rat race. And whoever keeps following all those unsuccessful people, will remain unsuccessful. But successful people handle each situation differently. Their point of view is different. That's why only a few people out of the huge population can be successful. Because they think, and act differently in every situation. If we have to overcome every situation and move forward smoothly, then we should think like successful people in every situation, good or bad.

Chapter 8

Doing things that are out of scope

DOING THINGS THAT ARE OUT OF SCOPE

"Greatness is living life outside of your comfort zone"-Lewis Howes.

Some people live with their dreams, and then they die with their dreams only. But can't make dreams come true. It's just because they don't know how to make dreams come true. If you live in a particular zone, you wake up in the morning and go to work and do your daily chores. But if your dreams are different from this lifestyle, then to turn your dreams into reality it is necessary to create the feeling of whatever you want in yourself. There are a few things you need to do to create this feeling by which gradually the belief will arise in you to get what you want. And when there is a belief then your desire will also be stronger. Then the necessary ideas will start coming to your mind to fulfil your dream. And you have to keep taking action according to your ideas. And beyond all prejudice, that dream of yours will turn into reality. There's no question that it shouldn't happen. Unless you develop some important feelings in you, you will not get the necessary motivation to take the necessary action. And also, you won't get the necessary ideas to take necessary action.

Suppose you want to go on a world tour one day. But you live in a poor locality and a very poor house. You do not have money; you are living very poorly. Everyone is like you in your locality or your friend circle. No one can even think of a world tour near you. Just because they do not have sufficient money and resources right now, that's why it is impossible according to their thinking and belief. So, they don't even try to mobilize the necessary resources. But if your dream is to go on a world tour, and looking at your situation, if you think that you can't do it. So your subconscious mind will accept it as true and will not give any new idea, and the result will be that you will not be able to fulfil your dream.

As our feelings and thoughts are, so are the things and situations we attract. First, you have to be in the frequency in which your dream is. To stay in that frequency, you have to awaken the feelings of your dreams within you.

To awaken that feeling inside you, you can do many things, like you can watch the videos of the world tour on the internet; you can see over the internet how people are roaming around, and enjoying the world tour. Then you can also take more information about ticket booking, hotel, flight booking. On social media, you can talk to people who have already gone on a world tour. Scrutinizing about all these things continuously will awaken a feeling in you, and then you will start to feel that you too fall into that category. The category of people who are going on a world tour. This feeling will give birth to belief. Because we easily believe only those things that we feel. And with belief, your desire will be stronger. And your desire will bring ideas into your mind that how you can achieve your goals very quickly and easily. And through those ideas, you will get that easy way, so that you will be able to fulfil your dream very soon. You have to act according to the ideas you get. After that, your old dream will turn into reality. Then you will find that what you found difficult for so many days has become very easy. In this way, you can turn any of your dreams into reality. The work seems very difficult before true belief and feeling, the same work seems easy after feeling and belief.

Chapter 9

Power of belief

POWER OF BELIEF

"Believe you can and you're halfway there"-Theodore Roosevelt

---

All the successful people you see in this world, no matter how hard they are working, can do that work successfully just because those people *believe* in that work. If anything works as a light in the dark, it is belief. Belief is the only thing that doesn't let a dying person die. Belief is the only solution to all despair. If you believe in something, no matter how big that thing is, you can achieve it. But the first step always starts with believing.

William Shakespeare put it in this way that our doubts are so treacherous that they make us too scared to try. And we lose on all fronts where we could have won. George Bernard Shaw says that people always blame their circumstances for their condition. But I don't believe in circumstances. The people who achieve success in this world are those who started the work and created their own desired circumstances. How pleasant is this reality, isn't it? And whoever believes in it has achieved success.

You get what you believe. So, before you can achieve any great success, you have to strongly believe that you can. Only then you can be successful. No work is possible or impossible; the only difference is belief. And whoever believes that this work is impossible for him then that work will seem impossible. Our minds will show millions of reasons why that work will be impossible. And if someone believes that this work is possible for him, then no matter how many obstacles he faces, no matter how tough that work may be, no matter how impossible that work may seem to others, he or she will do that work successfully sooner or later. There is no question that it should not be done. Like all the laws of nature, this rule is also accurate, believe and get whatever you want.

You have to believe in the unseen, no matter how difficult that situation may seem at first.

Chapter 10

Following own instincts

FOLLOWING OWN INSTINCTS

"Follow your instincts, that's where true wisdom manifest's itself"-Oprah Winfrey

Instinct is a subtle voice inside you. Whatever you do, your instincts are always showing you the right path. This voice knows what's right, and what's wrong for you. This voice knows everything. Where is the danger, Where is it safe, what is good for you, and what is bad for you. And it keeps showing you the right path throughout your life. Keeps warning of danger so that you can fix it in time. Like a guardian angel, it is always with you till you die.

Suppose your goal is to top the exam. So, if you want to achieve this goal, then you should focus on studying now. Instead, if you're busy playing video games right now, a subtle voice from within you will keep pushing you to study.

If you want to achieve anything in life, then you have to follow this voice all the time. Some people also call it the voice of the heart. All the people who have achieved success in this world have trusted this subtle voice. Great scientists, singers, businessmen, cricketers, doctors, actors became great, because they always relied on their instinct, and went ahead acting according to the same voice. The only problem is that some people do not follow this voice or do not understand this voice due to their lack of awareness.

The answers to all your questions are not outside you but inside you. If you look inside yourself and ask for an answer to any question, then you will get that answer for sure. With the help of meditation and yoga, you can understand your instinct better. If you follow your instinct and work every day accordingly, you will get success very easily.

Chapter 11

The idea is the real asset

THE IDEA IS THE REAL ASSET

"Everything begins with an idea"-Earl Nightingale

All the good things you see in this world, it was all in the form of an idea in someone's mind. And if all those people did not convert their ideas into actions, then all these materialistic things you are seeing in this world would not have happened. So, all the things you see in the form of an asset, i.e property, gold, shares, car and many things were all born out of an idea.

When you are looking for a solution to any problem, then you directly or indirectly ask your subconscious mind for the solution. Then your subconscious mind contacts with the infinite intelligence, and infinite intelligence through your subconscious mind give the solution to that problem in your conscious mind, that's what you call an idea. It works like a transmitter and a receiver. As such, by connecting to the satellite through a radio frequency transmitter, they have transmitted to the receiver i.e radio equipment. In the same way; our subconscious mind takes the solution to the problem from infinite intelligence, and transmits the solution to our conscious mind.

So, you have to protect every idea you get. If you are looking for a solution to any problem, and in the form of an idea if that solution flashes in your mind, then you have to convert that idea into action. Only then your problem can be solved. You can keep a pen and paper with you all the time. In which you can write down every thought, whatever comes to your mind. This will help you a lot to fulfil your goal. Billionaire Richard Branson said best of the entire thing that made him a billionaire is that he always kept a book and pen with him, and he used to write all his ideas on it daily. In this way, he protects his every idea. So later he can turn those ideas into action.

Chapter 12

How to get out of the pathetic situation

HOW TO GET OUT OF THE PATHETIC SITUATION

"No matter how pathetic the situation might be I'm sure of joy at the end. So be cheerful"-Kayode Seyi Tayo

---

No matter how bad the situation is, the truth is that you have created that situation yourself. You may be surprised to read this but it is true. You are in this situation because of your thoughts, your feelings, and your beliefs. God did not put you in this situation. Neither your luck put you in this situation, nor does your government put you in this situation. No matter how bad the economic condition of your country is, no matter how poor your family is, if you are not living the way you want to live at this time, then this situation was created because of you. If you want to change your situation, first of all, you have to change your way of thinking, and your attitude. You have to be aware of what you pay attention to. Whatever you pay maximum attention to throughout the day, your situation becomes more and more similar.

Suppose you have very little money in your bank account right now, and if you keep thinking that 'I am poor, I have less money, I can't do this, I can't do that, it's not my thing, my salary is so low' etc, so you will continue to live more such life, and it's hardly possible that your life will ever be better. If you want to get out of this situation then you should think about your dream life. And you should not think about what is happening in your life right now. When the desire for the desired increases, the unwanted ends.

Suppose, if you want to create a good business but right now you are doing some simple job, which you do not like to do. So, you should think about that business. Should think about how to start the business successfully, how to arrange initial investment. But you should not think negatively like I can never do this business or this is not my cup of tea etc.

We can understand this process in 3 simple steps:

1st step

You need to visualize your goal with all your senses and you have to feel the happiness that you will feel when you live the life of your dreams.

2nd step

You have to act on every effective idea that comes to your mind.

3rd step

When you proceed by acting according to those thoughts, you will have to express the deepest gratitude to the Infinite intelligence for receiving every little thing.

After that, no matter how bad a situation you are in, that situation will start to change. And you won't even know when you will enter the life sphere of your dreams.

Chapter 13

When you initiate it becomes easier

WHEN YOU INITIATE IT BECOMES EASIER

"Everything is initially difficult before they become easy"—Thomas Fuller

When you want to do some work but you don't, the more days you go by not doing that work, the more difficult it becomes for you to do that work. But once you start doing that work, then no matter how tough that work is, that work becomes easy for you. Fear disappears from our minds after taking the initiative. We start feeling confident after we initiate.

Most people have a habit of procrastination. They keep postponing every important work. The result is that time flies and important opportunities are missed.

Some people create many opportunities by using their will and imagination. But when it comes to taking action, they do procrastinate. Because of that, they fail. You can eliminate the habit of procrastination by taking initiative in any work. Because after taking the initiative, the work seems easy.

We can understand this with an example, suppose you want to wake up at 5 in the morning and you are not able to wake up so early. So if you usually get up at 9, just set a goal to get up 10 minutes earlier, as soon as you take the initiative, you will sooner or later hit your goal.

Chapter 14

The glasses you wear become the world you stare at

THE GLASSES YOU WEAR BECOME THE WORLD YOU STARE AT

"Don't call the world dirty because you forgot to clean your glasses"-Aaron Hill

The way you look at any situation, you will see that situation like that only. We can understand this with an example, suppose you have 4 friends, and all your friends have been kept wearing glasses of different colours. Someone wears yellow, someone wears white, someone wears black, and someone wears red. If you all come out of the house, then you will see all the things around you, according to the colour of your glasses. But the question is what the fact is? Fact is what you will see by taking off your glasses. In the same way, we all keep glasses of different colours in our minds. And that is, we all have different beliefs about the same thing or situations. We all react differently to a particular situation. But the truth can only be one. This belief is created by seeing the masses and trusting the things heard that we don't even know. To overcome this, the first thing you can do is ask questions to see each situation as it is. Every superstition, every myth exists in this world just because most people don't get to the root of them. You can ask like this. If this is so, why is it? 'I'm thinking so, but why?' 'What is the base behind my attitude towards it?' When you ask yourself such questions, then automatically you will start seeing the facts of everything. Then the glasses will be removed from your mind, and you will be able to see everything crystal clear. Then, you will see only truth, nothing else.

Chapter 15

Staying inspired

STAYING INSPIRED

"Choose to be inspired"-Joe Rogan

Why is it important to stay inspired?

Any goal cannot be achieved without inspiration. You should be inspired in every situation. When you think of achieving anything big, it will always conflict with your present situation.

Suppose you want to be a big businessman or a billionaire, but now you are too poor. So, if you do not have enough inspiration, you won't get the energy you need to take the necessary actions every day. This means without inspiration you will be mentally very lazy, and you can't do anything with full focus. When you are inspired, you get a push from within to do any work. With Inspiration, you don't have to force yourself to do anything. You take action on your own and take a lot more action than before. Whenever you feel that you cannot do any work, then you should take the help of inspiration.

You can listen to inspirational songs in your free time. Reading a biography of successful people or knowing about them on the internet will inspire you more. If you try to find out in your spare time, that how any successful person achieves success, what are the difficulties he has to face, and despite that how do they move forward? And if you keep listening or reading all this every day, then inspiration will arise in you too. You will be filled with a different spirit. Then nothing called Impossible will exist for you. Your inspiration will be at its peak. Then anyone's negative thoughts or comments will not have any effect on you. No great achievement can be possible without any inspiration.

Chapter 16

Always be happy

ALWAYS BE HAPPY

"Happiness is not a goal. It's a by-product of a life well lived"-Eleanor Roosevelt

---

Why is it necessary to be happy?

Eventually, we are happy when we get something or when we get what we want. But happiness should not be the result of getting something; it is a state of mind. When you are happy, you live in that frequency in which all good things happen. It is your choice whether you will be in a happy state of mind or not. Often people become happy or unhappy because of the circumstances. But in reality, it is the reverse. Your condition is bad so you are not unhappy; rather, you are unhappy so your condition is bad. But if you're unhappy it also means you're unsatisfied. The longer you stay in this unsatisfied state of mind, the more you slow down your progress. In this unsatisfied state of mind, your brain doesn't work properly. Then it becomes difficult to find solutions to your problems. Then your circumstances gradually get worse and you are prone to think that your luck is getting worse.

When you are completely happy & joyful then your mind and body can work at their peak. And you can find solutions to any problems very effectively. Then good thoughts start coming to your mind, and it becomes very easy to get the things you want.

How to always be happy?

There is a reason behind every unhappy moment. If you repeatedly seek the cause of your unhappy state of mind, and if you make that cause in your mind too small, then you will return to a happy state of mind. When you keep doing this, again and again, you will realize how difficult it is to be unhappy, and how easy it is to be happy.

No matter what the worst experience you have in your life, if right now it is not in your hands to fix it then it is pointless to feel worried about it. Because remorse is a negative emotion. If you have a negative attitude about a problem then other problems may arise. Because you are in the same frequency as you feel, you will continue to attract similar situations in your life. Then due to not having your full attention in the present, you will not be able to focus on the solution to the problems. And your problems will continue to grow. When you feel anxious or scared, you are not able to fully focus on the present moment. The result will be that you keep going backwards in your life, and you miss important opportunities.

Sometimes due to a particular situation our state of mind automatically changes. And suddenly we start reacting differently, which we don't even realize. Whenever we start feeling negative away from our positive feelings, we have to question ourselves. 'Why am I reacting like this?' 'What is the reason?' Then you can stay in a happy state of mind by negating that reason.

In any situation, we all react according to our state of mind. So we have to identify our state of mind, only then we can change it to reach a happy state of mind.

We often live with this myth that, 'I will be happy if my dream will come true or after getting a lot of money, or after getting my favourite life partner I want. But the truth is that most people are not happy even after getting all they want. First of all, we have to find our inner happiness, and then all these things will be able to give us true happiness. When you are in a happy state of mind, it acts as fuel to get you anything. That means, the progress of your life also depends on your happiness. Can you remember the name of any billionaire who is unhappy with his life? It doesn't happen often. Because our happiness has a direct relation with our progress.

So don't just *wish* to be happy, *choose* to be happy.

Chapter 17

Desire is the first point of every achievement

DESIRE IS THE FIRST POINT OF EVERY ACHIEVEMENT

"The starting point of all achievement is a desire"-Napolean hill

Desire is the first point of every invention. Desire is the thing due to which whatever has been invented in the world today, has become possible. If there was no desire to do anything in anyone, then whatever comfortable life we are living today, we would not be able to live the same life. And whatever development you see in this world now, you could not see that. If you have a burning desire to do something, then it means that you have a lot of power to do that work. Only it is necessary to develop that work by taking necessary action. We all have different desires in this world. We all act according to different desires. And we live as we desire. You also have to have a great desire to achieve great success. If you do some work for which you have no desire, then you can never get the greatest success in that work. We see most of the people all around us unhappy with their work and their life. Just because they go on doing those things throughout their life, they do not have the slightest desire. They are just doing it for the money. That's why you should always choose the work which you have the desire.

For a person who has a great desire for anything, his success is equally great.

Chapter 18

The ambience is important

THE AMBIENCE IS IMPORTANT

"Fill your ambience with excellence"-
Anyaele sam chiyson

Your ambience has a profound effect on your thinking, and your belief system. We can understand this with an example. Suppose you have seen a lot of wealth since childhood. Most of the day you have breakfast in Switzerland and have lunch in New York, and that's how you become 25 years old. You stay with rich people 24 hours a day. There is always talking of prosperity, and wealth in your home and office. Despite living in such an ambience for 24 hours, if I tell you that you will become very poor one day, will you believe me? No way. Why so? Because you are not living in a poor ambience, so you won't believe it at all. We believe more in such things than what we see and hear. Just like, if you live 24 hours in such an environment where all the negative people live around you. Where you only hear that you are not capable of doing this, you are not in a position to earn that much money, you are too poor. Or you live in such an environment, that you hear ordinary people around you saying that they are poor or middle-class people, it is not their thing to earn big money or become very rich or do something big. Or they feel that inflation has become so much that they are not able to move forward even if they want. If you live in this ambience every day and if you hear and believe all these negative talks every day, then no matter how many people come and say that you can become rich or whatever your goal is, you can achieve it, then you will not believe it. Just like the rich person, around whom all the positive ambience is there, that's why he ignores the talks of poverty. What we see and hear every day has a profound effect on our minds. And slowly when it becomes our belief at the subconscious level, we do not even know it.

Ways to avoid it

Whenever you live in such an ambience that leaves a negative impression in your mind, and whenever you meet people who look for problems in every solution, stay away from such ambience, and such people. Such people can be your relatives, friends or even in your family.

Staying away does not mean that you stop talking to them completely, and leave one place and go to another place. But you can talk to them at least. Whenever they talk negatively you can change the topic. You can constantly focus on your positive belief and your goal. And you can be fully determined. You can avoid a place where there are only negative things or talks around. You can avoid any negative places or things that may mislead your belief system.

Chapter 19

The feeling of abundance

THE FEELING OF ABUNDANCE

"Abundance is not something we acquire.

It is something we tune into"—Wayne dyer

This universe works on science and laws. Often you will hear people saying this, 'the rich are getting richer day by day, and the poor are getting poorer'. It's because those people constantly feel the same. The rich feel like the rich, and the poor feel like the poor, so they become more like what they feel. When someone has money, they have the feeling of money. So they attract more money. And on the contrary, the one who is short of money, and if his whole focuses are on scarcity, then because of the feeling of lack, he always attracts the shortage. Empty pockets cannot easily attract money. Therefore, no matter how bad our situation is, we should never empty our wallets or bank accounts. Because then the feeling of the money goes, and the feeling of lack comes. We need to save money for the feeling of abundance. That's why whatever you earn; you must save 10% of your earnings. People often save the money they have after spending. But if you want to remain wealthy for the rest of your life, and want to live a happy life, then you should think about saving before spending. You might not have enough money to save; your income may be too low. Even if your income is as low as 100 rupees, then you must save 10 per cent i.e. 10 rupees. Right now these 10 rupees may make you look small, but after some time, you will have a lot of money accumulated by adding such 10 rupees. Then you will find that saving amount very big. When you have enough money, you should invest that money somewhere, so that you can get good returns for that invested amount. This will increase your wealth. And then whatever return you get out of that invested amount, it should be reinvested. In doing so, you will never go back to the ranks of poverty again. That's how you can put your money to work. Then your money will earn you money.

But while doing all this, you have to pay special attention to your expenses. All wasteful expenditure will have to be cut away until you make so much money, that whatever you spend out of it, your money will never be less.

We can understand this with an example. Suppose you sow a mango tree, you took good care of that tree, gave water, the tree grew, and then a couple of fruits came. And you didn't pluck the fruits. Then a lot of fruit came on that tree. Yet you have not plucked the fruits. Then you sowed the seed of that fruit again. Due to this, so many trees were formed that the whole land was filled with trees. Now you are taking good care of so many trees too. And when this whole mango orchard will bear fruit, then whatever fruit you pluck, it is such a big orchard that you will not be able to finish it all. And with each passing day, the trees and fruits will continue to grow. You have to do the same thing with your money.

Chapter 20

Changing habits faster

CHANGING HABITS FASTER

"Your habits will determine your future"-
Jack Canfield

What will you achieve in life, what will you become, how will you live, how much money you will earn, it all will be decided by your habits. People often want to win by defeating other people to get success. But to achieve great success, in reality, you need to win by fighting with yourself, and not fighting with others. There is a need to fight every bad habit that comes between you and your success.

How and why?

Suppose you are a very healthy person, and you want to lose weight. And your daily habit is like, you wake up at 11 am, then you take 1 cup of coffee, then you take a heavy diet, after some time you take junk food. And even after maintaining this routine, if you are thinking wildly every day that you have to lose weight, you are not doing anything to change your habit. You are getting upset every day because of your weight. And you'll start thinking,

'Maybe it's god's will that I will always be overweight', 'I will probably never be able to lose weight ' etc. And thus, with each passing day, you will be more and more concerned about your obesity. But you will not even realize that your habit is responsible for all these things.

How to change your habits?

Our brain is a very complex machine. And this brain is programmed in a particular way with some habits, beliefs and thought processes, just like a computer. When a computer runs in a particular operating system, that computer will have programming related to that operating system only. If it is tried to run according to other operating systems, it will not work. Unless another operating system is inserted in that computer after doing full formatting. So is our brain. If a particular brain is programmed with a particular thought process, beliefs, and habits, and when we try to change our habits or belief then we feel mental pressure, and adrenaline and cortisol hormones are released, and we become anxious. Our mind feels that we are leaving our comfort zone, and entering an uncomfortable zone. And the mind does not like an uncomfortable zone. Due to not understanding this thing, most people are not able to change their habits throughout their life, and go on with those bad habits; the result is that they remain unsuccessful. If our mind is not engaged in any important work, our mind will always find that thing that is very easy and which is fun to do. Because doing fun activities releases dopamine. Dopamine is a hormone that is released when we do something fun that we enjoy doing.

If you wake up in the morning and think of exercising, then this is unpleasant work for the mind, the mind will immediately refuse you to do that work, the result will be that you will not be able to move forward. You will not be able to do the important work that should be done. And you will start thinking that why you are failing again and again. There is a simple way to win by fighting with your mind.

Divide your task

You can divide your task into as small parts as possible. After that, if you complete these small parts, then dopamine will be released, your mind will be happy, and will motivate you to do more.

Suppose you want to exercise in the morning, then first of all focus on getting up in the morning. If you wake up at 9 am, then set a goal of getting up at 8:30 am, Getting up at 8 am the next day, getting up the next day at 7:30, and getting up the next day at 7 o'clock, and continue like that. Dopamine will continue to be released in your mind as you complete that day's goal with each passing day. Whenever your brain feels that any difficult task has been completed, it releases dopamine. Because your mind likes that you will not have to do that difficult task anymore because it's over. When one goal is achieved, like getting up in the morning, then focus on the other goals, like exercising. You have to do the same in doing exercise too. If you want to hit pushups, then on the first day just set a target of 1 pushup, 2nd day 2 pushups, and 3rd day 3 like this. If you try to change your every habit part by part, then you will be surprised to see that you have achieved your goal very soon. In this way, your mind will support you in everything. And you will be able to change your life by changing any habit. You may also feel anxious when you try to change your habits. This is because you were living with these bad habits for so many years, and now you are going to be completely transformed. Because synaptic connections are made in our brain in the way we think and believe. When we try to change our habits, those synaptic connections start to break down. So, it seems tough and very hardworking to change any habit. That's why our brain prevents us from changing our habits. In this situation, most people give up the effort and fail. As if your mind will be telling you 'Why are you doing this, you can't do that much'. But you shouldn't listen to your mind. You have to keep trying to change your habit for 21 days. If you keep changing any habit for 21 days, it will change.

Make a list of all your bad habits that you need to change. Then target a habit, and try to change it continuously for 21 days. And when you feel that you have overcome it, then try to change the other habit. Keeping your dream in mind always will make you change habits easily.

Whenever you feel like giving up this effort, think about your dreams and tell yourself that if you want to reach your goal then you have to complete this work anyway. Then you will get so much motivation that you will change all your bad habits very soon. When you completely replace all your bad habits with your good habits, then when you look back, you will wonder how pointless you were living before.

Along with your new habits, new beliefs will also arise, and along with new beliefs, you will also have to take new steps.

Thinking habit

Just as there are habits to work, and live life, in the same way, you also have a habit of thinking. Your life's habits depend on your thinking habits. How you think and what you believe in, determines your Habits. So, to change every bad habit in your life, you have to change your thinking habits first.

Suppose you want to do a business, but you are not taking any new steps every day to run this business, and you keep going with your old habits. It's just because your thinking habit is not right. Maybe you have some doubts about whether this business will work or not. You're not completely confident about your beliefs. So, unless you change the bad habits of thinking, you will not be able to change your physical bad habits either.

We think like that, 'I had tried before but nothing happened. So this time too it won't happen'. But we do not realize that there is much difference between this time and last time. We are no longer what we were before. Now everything has changed. When we do not consider ourselves capable, then laziness dominates us.

Chapter 21

Destroying all triggers

DESTROYING ALL TRIGGERS

"Root out the problem before the problem kills you"-Acharya Chanakya

When you start walking on a new path by changing your thinking, beliefs, way of doing things, and habits, then you may find some old signs step by step. We can call these signs triggers. Triggers that can reactivate your old bad habits. And because of that, you won't even know when you'll reach the old surface again.

You must have seen many people around you who want and try a lot to change their current situation and their life. But they fail because they remain entangled in the triggers.

Music, videos, your old clothes, some places, some people, some apps, all these can be triggers for you.

You can stop listening to that music or watching the videos you used to listen to when you were living an unwanted life, detached from the desired life of the current situation. You can talk less to some people who remind you of your old life again and again. Your clothes can be a trigger. The clothes you used to wear before the transformation. You can keep your clothes out of sight. Some apps you can uninstall from your phone if they are triggers according to you, which reminded you again and again of your old habits and way of living your old life. Similarly, you can avoid those things that you think may be a trigger. We can understand this with an example. Suppose you have just turned from a fat man to a completely healthy man, then Junk food can be a trigger for you now. Maybe you sometimes feel like eating junk food by seeing it, so you have to ignore the places where you always have junk food in front of your eyes. You can avoid watching any such videos where they are telling about tasty food. Because it may be the triggers and you can start eating such unhealthy food again because of these triggers. And you can also uninstall any food app from your phone, because seeing that app may make you feel like ordering unhealthy food. Or if you have all your old oversized clothes in front of your eyes, then this may be a trigger for you. By which you can become lazy again, and can reduce exercise, and can return to the old habits again.

If you always protect yourself from these types of triggers, you will feel that you are completely in a new life, and completely transformed. In this way, you can say goodbye to all your bad habits, and unwanted situations permanently.

Chapter 22

Effective work is supreme

EFFECTIVE WORK IS SUPREME

"Dreams don't work unless you do"-John
C Maxwell

As you sow so shall you reap. Like all the laws of nature, there is a law of cause and effect, and no one can change it. This specifically states that every single action in the universe produces a reaction no matter what. And it works equally for everybody in this world.

Science has made a lot of progress but nothing has been developed so far that we can get something without doing anything. You can bring opportunities to you by thinking about the things you want, and you get them by taking action. No one can get anything without paying the price. You have to serve. How much will be your income, will depend on your service. If you want to increase your income, then you have to increase your service. And if you want less income then you have to reduce your service too. You will make money only when you give service worth it.

But you must have seen many such people, who are unable to achieve anything even after doing a lot of hard work. And some people achieve a lot even by doing a little work. This is because some people always work ineffectively; On the contrary, some people always do everything effectively.

You can't get everything just by working hard, you have to work effectively. Right place, right timing, and the right job, all three should be in sync. There are two types of work, effective and ineffective. If you do your daily tasks ineffectively then you will remain unsuccessful. And if you always do everything effectively, then nothing can stop you from achieving success. The result of every effective work is cumulative. You have to work in a particular way in the direction you want to go according to your instinct. Some people ineffectively do a lot of work, and they are not able to succeed in it. The reason for success is the result of doing enough things effectively, and not doing any work ineffectively.

To create a lot of wealth, most people do a lot of business ineffectively. Due to this, they think that doing more business will bring more money, but it is not true. Instead, if they do one business effectively enough, that same business can make them a lot of wealth.

You should always do the work which you do not feel like work but an easy game. You should do a work in which you are interested, only then can you achieve the greatest achievement in that work. No man can achieve the greatest success in a work he is not passionate about. Your interest in any work is proof that you have the full potential to do that work.

Chapter 23

Morning routine

MORNING ROUTINE

"Your Morning Routine generates a 10x return for good or for bad. Make it good"-Todd Stocker.

Early to bed and early to rise makes a man healthy wealthy and wise. We all have heard this quote at least once in our lifetime. But does anyone know why? Why sleep early, waking up early can make you healthy, wealthy & wise? Most billionaires are morning persons. Because they know very well the benefits of waking up in the morning. When you wake up between 5 and 6 in the morning, then the climate remains clear. The air remains very pure. Then your logical mind is turned off. Due to this, you do not overthink. And then you can easily put your goals or dreams in your subconscious mind. In the early morning, there is silence all around, due to this you can do any work without distraction.

Step by step we can complete our morning routine:

1st

Make your bed

The first thing you should do when you wake up is fixing your bed. Some people find this work very useless. But this work is very important for your productivity throughout the day. Because when you fix your bed, then the mind gets the impression that the first task has been completed. Then your mind will motivate you to complete other tasks as well throughout the day.

2nd

Meditation

It is our human nature, as soon as we wake up in the morning, we start searching for our present reality. We start to recollect who I am, and where am I living. How much money is there in my bank account? What good or bad happened to me yesterday, or what good or bad can happen to me today? Thinking of all these thoughts, we become stressed or panic. And the result is that our whole day goes bad, wasted and demotivated.

That is why, by doing meditation in the morning, our minds become calm and relaxed. That's why we can focus well on any work, and can easily complete all the tasks of our day.

3rd

Affirmation

Affirmations are a very powerful tool to remind your subconscious mind about your goal over and over again. You can record positive affirmations to achieve your goals. And if you hear those affirmations early in the morning, your subconscious mind remembers what goals you have to work for during the day. You stay focused all day, you remember your goals during the day, so you do any work with more dedication, and you can complete that work without any distraction.

4th

Journal

Whatever you write, you can remember it very easily, which cannot be done by just thinking. You can write a to-do list for the whole day. You can write about your goals, dreams, which you want to achieve in future, and near future. You can completely analyze your goals. How close you have reached your goals so far, how much is left, how many more days will it take you to complete the rest of the goals, what resources may be needed to complete your goals, everything you can analyze. This will prepare a complete map in your mind of what exactly you need to do to achieve your goals.

5th

Imagination

When you imagine your goals in the morning with all your senses, then from the morning you live in the frequency in which your goals are. Because of this your subconscious mind will keep bringing the right ideas to your mind and will keep motivating you to do the right things throughout the day. Because of this, you will do only effective work throughout the day so that your goal can be fulfilled very soon.

6th

Exercise

Exercising in the morning brings a different energy to our mind and body for the whole day. Hormones like adrenaline, and cortisol, are not released due to exercise, which hormones create fear in our body. Due to the non-release of these hormones, we feel completely confident, energized, and fit throughout the day. That's why we can do any work very effectively.

7th

Wake up your inspiration

You cannot achieve any great success without inspiration. You can do any work effectively only when you are fully inspired towards that work or your goal. It is very important to wake up our inspiration in the morning so that we can stay inspired during the whole day's work.

To awaken the inspiration, you can read a self-help book. You can read a biography of a great person or you can watch any inspiring videos on the internet so that your inspiration will be on top for the whole day.

Chapter 24

Erasing the past

ERASING THE PAST

"The past cannot be cured"-Elizabeth L

Some people always live in the past. They wake up in the morning; do their daily chores, but not effectively. Because they are always in past troubles, like anger over one's actions in past, vengeance with someone, loss of money, betrayal in love, and many more. Or they remain sad because of the troubles of the immediate past. That's why they often say that nothing is going well with me these days. And in the same way, because of feeling negative by staying in the past every day, they are always in low frequency. Because of this, they are not able to achieve anything special. Because they do work in the present but their attention is always on the past. The result is that their progress slows down. Disappointment, self-aggrandizement, guilt, vengeance, fear, all these feelings weaken us. How we feel has a profound effect on our progress.

The one, who is always in the past, keeps connecting himself with that past every day. The result is that the same past becomes their identity, and their whole life ends by getting entangled in that past.

We should learn from the mistakes of the past but should not carry them with us continuously. Because no matter how hard we try, we cannot fix our past.

By setting your favourite goal and working towards it, you can forget the past completely, and start over again.

You can turn to meditation to let go of negative feelings that repeatedly drag you back to the past.

Chapter 25

Stretching the limits

STRETCHING THE LIMITS

"The only limits in our life are those we impose on ourselves"-Bob Proctor

The more you stretch your limits, the more you will achieve. There is a total of 7.9 billion people in this world; everyone has different interests and different desires. Similarly, everyone has different limits. And when their limit is reached, and they are satisfied, they try not to exceed it; the result is that they do not even get more than that, and they are stuck only for a small limit. We have to stretch our limits all the time. Many people stop when they achieve the smallest goal they set, and don't put in much effort for a bigger goal. Because that small goal looks like a big goal to them.

How to stretch your limits?

To stretch your limits also, you can think like a successful person. As if will Mr Bill Gates or Mr Elon Musk or Mr Sachin Tendulkar be happy at such a small achievement? If the answer is no, then ask yourself, why would I stop achieving after this? By continuously increasing your limits, you can achieve such a big goal, which you did not even expect earlier.

Chapter 26

Valuing precious time

VALUING PRECIOUS TIME

"Time and tide wait for none"-Geoffrey Chaucer.

All the good things you have right now are important because you have time. We can achieve whatever we want in this world, no matter how big or how small, but time is limited for all of us. We all have come from somewhere, and we all have to leave here one day. The time in between is limited for everyone. Often people say that I am having a bad time that is just because those people are not making better use of their time. We should make better use of our time every day so that we can reach our greatest potential.

We all will die one day. People always think they have a lot of time. But suddenly one day they feel that they wasted a lot of time, and didn't use it very well. We should manage our time every day, and make the best use of it. Because this is the only thing that is getting less and less from our life with every second. And we can never get it back. We should invest as much time as possible in our life, reaching our greatest potential. That's why we came to this world. No matter what age you are, you can start again. The best time to start was yesterday. And the second-best time to start is now.

Chapter 27

To be curious

TO BE CURIOUS

"I have no special talent I am only passionately curious"-
Albert Einstein.

Whenever you start moving towards your dream life, Then you often fall into misconceptions. To rise from those misconceptions, you have to ask a question at every step. You can go deep into anything just by asking questions. If you're curious enough, there's no question you can't find an answer to. We are often told from childhood that do not ask too many questions. This is so because; they also did not ask many questions to anyone in their life span. And even if they did, they must have heard the same thing from their elders that do not ask more questions. As a result, they also got half-knowledge only. Many people do not know the answer to too many questions. It's just because, they are not so curious enough to go to the end of anything. They don't ask questions. They just guess apart from knowing unknown things. They believe without knowing anything exactly. And by doing so they are unable to face the truth most of the time. You may not find the answer to any of the questions even after searching a lot. But you have to stick to that question until you get an answer. You should not ignore any question without getting a proper answer. Many people know only incomplete, apart from knowing anything completely. And later this half-knowledge is of no use to them.

The answer to the questions could be found anywhere, through the internet, through anyone, elder or younger or even from a kid. You have to look for your answer everywhere. Only then can you get the right answer from the right source. Some people ask questions, but they do not get their answers from the right source. Because of this, they misunderstand the wrong information coming from the wrong source as the correct information. If you want to reach your greatest potential then you have to question everything step by step. There cannot be a problem that cannot be solved, and there cannot be a question that cannot be answered.

Chapter 28

The miraculous effect of celibacy

THE MIRACULOUS EFFECT OF CELIBACY

"Celibacy is a great help in as much as it enables one to live a life of full surrender to god"-Mahatma Gandhi

Celibacy means abstention from sexual relations. Often, whenever we see a successful person, we say that he is a successful person. When seeing an unsuccessful person, we say that he is a failure. But we never even try to find out, why any person was successful or unsuccessful? There are many factors behind someone being successful or unsuccessful. One of them is Celibacy. And that's a huge factor. Whoever has achieved great success must have followed *celibacy* knowingly or unknowingly.

Sex energy is the energy, from which a living being can be born. Who laughs, cries, talks, walks, wins the competition, and invents wonderful things in this world. But this human being who is the best among all living beings is born with just a little sex energy. So now we can understand that if this miraculous energy stays inside our body, then how many wonderful things it can do. When people follow celibacy, they have an amazing power to take action. And then they get involved in the work in such a way as if a hungry person yearns for food: All their attention automatically starts on the important things. And they start working, and their development starts. The human brain is driven by emotion. With positive emotions, the brain interacts with the supreme Intelligence more intensely by entering higher rates of vibrations. The most powerful emotion among all the emotions is the feeling of sexual energy.

It's a bountiful power. If you do not use this energy for any specific purpose, it will find some lower exit, and demand physical manifestation. Due to not understanding this thing, many people fail to reach their greatest potential.

When you follow celibacy, then you also start getting answers to all those questions, which you were not able to get earlier. Then your brain starts working at its highest potential. In the absence of this energy, our brain is not able to work so efficiently.

If we consider our brain as a car, then the car will not be able to run properly, unless the right fuel is put in it. Sex energy is like the right fuel for our brain, due to which our brain starts working at a faster rate. With, this energy we can see beyond every horizon where there was only darkness before. Sex energy is creative energy, when you use this energy in any work; you become more creative than before. With celibacy, your instinct becomes more powerful.

Just as one can achieve great success by following celibacy knowingly or unknowingly, similarly one cannot achieve great success unless one follows *celibacy*. Most people don't have the greatest success before the age of 40. As most people before the age of 40 engage more in physical expression. Abraham Lincoln also had great success only after the age of 40 years. There are examples of millions of great people who got the greatest success only after the age of 40. Because, after the age of 40 most people get bored with physical attachments. And because of that, people knowingly or unknowingly follow celibacy. And they become focused on their work many times more than before. And they keep on developing.

Chapter 29

Miracles of meditation

MIRACLES OF MEDITATION

"Meditation is the only magic in the world and the only miracle"-Osho

The most successful people you see in this world are doing their job very successfully. They can do their job successfully because; they pay enough attention to every aspect of their work. You can do any work very successfully, only when you give enough attention to every aspect of any work. To pay proper attention, your awareness must be on top. Better awareness comes from meditation. If you want to reach your goal very fast, then meditation is the easiest way. If you want to do hours of work in minutes, then meditation is the easiest way. Your pineal gland gets activated when you meditate daily. The result is that you stay away from stress and anger. And your anxiety and stress disappear like it was never before. You become very calm and relaxed. Your brain can only function to its full potential when it is in a relaxed state. You can get the solution to your every problem very effectively, only when your brain is in a relaxed state. Your instinct works well with meditation. With meditation, you can take more and more correct decisions. So, the result will be, that your life will also start going in the right direction. You will not be afraid to make decisions in any new situation. Then no work remains big or small for you. Everything seems easy. You start trying new things. When you do daily meditation you do not panic even in the worst situations. And you can understand every aspect of life in detail. When you do deep meditation, then your brain goes into the alpha stage. In that stage all the creativity takes place. When you are in that state then you do everything creatively. when you are in a meditative state then a tough situation can be easily solved. You get a different way of understanding with meditation.

Chapter 30

Benefits of yoga

BENEFITS OF YOGA

"To perform every action artfully is yoga"-Swami Kripalu

Great success can never be achieved with a tired body and mind, nor can a tired body and mind lead a happy life. That's why we must practice yoga. Yoga provides a good geometry to our body and mind. By which we are connected to the whole universe. We can understand our instincts better. Our every sense works well. If you incorporate yoga practice into your discipline every day, your mind and body will function in a much better way. There will be proper oxygen flow to every cell of your body and mind. And you will feel energized all day long. You will not feel tired easily. Your strength will be better than before. When your body and mind are full of oxygen, you will feel better throughout the day. And you'll have a good night's sleep too. Yoga practices keep you fit and disease-free, and keep you healthy, which greatly reduces your chances of getting diseases. Due to this, you save a lot of time, which was earlier wasted due to illness.

Some popular yoga practices are pranayam, shirshasan etc.

CONCLUSION

A lot of people read thousands of such books. After reading they understand a lot. But even after that, they do not apply those methods in their life. And their lives remain the same. You have to apply every method mentioned in this book in your life. Only then can you change your life completely, and can live your dream life forever.

In the first chapter, we learned how we get stuck in a loop because of our belief system. And our lives go on in the same loop. How do we get stuck in loops again and again due to the programming of our minds. If we want to get out of this loop, then we have to change the programming of our minds.

In Chapter 2 we learned, how to always be in a positive vibration by expressing our gratitude towards the Almighty, by which we can easily get anything faster.

In Chapter 3 we learned, how we get what we think about. Apart from that, whatever things we criticize, we create more in our life.

In Chapter 4 we learned that our outer world or outer circumstances have started from inside our mind i.e. inner world. This means we can also change the external circumstances by fixing our inner minds or creating the world of the things we want inside the mind.

In Chapter 5 we learned, how we can achieve anything by imagining the things we want crystal clear in our minds. Imagination is a glimpse of the circumstances to come. When we imagine anything or a situation, we embody it.

In Chapter 6 we learned, what Subconscious Mind is. What is the work of the subconscious mind and how can we use the power of our subconscious mind.

In Chapter 7 we learned, how successful people think. How can we think like the successful people of this world in every situation, and will be able to make the decisions like them. So sooner or later, we can also become successful.

In Chapter 8, we learned, how we can fulfil our dream by thinking and feeling different from our current situation, and we also learned how important is the feeling of anything that we want to get the thing easily.

In Chapter 9, we learned, how by believing we can make the impossible possible. When we do not have anything, if we believe in our dreams, we can achieve them. No matter how big it is.

In Chapter 10 we learned, what are Instincts. Instincts keep giving us signals throughout our life as to what is right for us. And if we want to achieve anything, then we have to work according to this subtle voice inside us.

In Chapter 11 we learned, that our ideas are the biggest asset. We should protect our every idea and move ahead by taking action according to those ideas.

In Chapter 12, we learned that no matter how many pathetic situations we live in, we can come out of that situation and live the life we want.

In Chapter 13, we learned how we can make any task easier by taking initiative. And until we do not initiate any work, it seems difficult.

In Chapter 14, we learned that the way we look at this world, this world looks the same way. We all see different situations in different ways, but the fact is only one. So, we can see this fact by correcting the bias and beliefs of our minds.

In Chapter 15, we learned why we should stay inspired. And what can we do to stay inspired? Whenever our situation is against our wish, then how can we create the situation we want by staying inspired?

In Chapter 16 we learned that being happy is very important. And there is a direct connection between happiness and our progress.

In Chapter 17 we learned that desire is the first point of our success. If no one has any desire to do anything, so there won't be any good things in this world that could exist that exist now.

In Chapter 18 we learned, how our ambience has a profound effect on our success. What is most important is, in what ambience we live in.

In Chapter 19 we learned, how to have a feeling of abundance is important for us to become wealthy. Because empty pockets can't attract money. And we also learned how we can become much wealthier by reinvesting our money.

In Chapter 20 we learned how our habits are responsible for our success. How we don't fix our habits even if we want to, and always be unsuccessful. And we learned how we can easily change our habits.

In Chapter 21 we learned that if we have to change our habits completely and live a completely new life, we have to stay away from some triggers or else we may reach the old path again.

In Chapter 22 we learned, that no matter what we think, we have to take necessary actions, only then will be able to live the life we want, and can get anything.

In Chapter 23 we learned, how our morning routine should be. So that we can take action effectively throughout the day.

In Chapter 24 we learned that if we are always stuck in our past, we will never be able to take necessary actions in the present. According to this, we will not even be able to make a good future.

In Chapter 25 we learned how to keep on stretching our limits every step of the way to achieve great success.

In Chapter 26 we learned that we can achieve whatever we want in our lives, but time is limited for all of us. That's why we should use time wisely.

In Chapter 27 we learned that as we move forward to achieve great achievements, many challenges will come before us. That's why we should be curious. Only then we will be able to effectively solve every problem.

In Chapter 28 we learned, how by the following celibacy we can achieve great success in every aspect of our life, which is not possible without celibacy.

In Chapter 29 we learned how useful meditation can be, to do any work effectively.

In Chapter 30 we learned, what changes can come to our mind and body through yoga. Due to this many effective changes can occur in our thinking ability and the way of working.

Somebody becomes successful not because he has good luck. Somebody becomes successful because he has chosen to be like that -Surajit Chakravarty.

Best of ~~luck~~ Choices.

Thank you

Thank you for taking the time to read *Live Out Of The Zone.* I hope that you found the information useful. Just remember, that a key part of the learning process is putting what you read into practice.

If you enjoy reading this book then consider putting a review on amazon.

Also, if you have any questions, comments, or feedback about this book, you can send me a message, and I will get back to you as soon as possible. My email address is:

reyanshchakravarty01@gmail.com